Echoes of Love

Echoes of Love

Effervescent Memories

Charles R. Lanham

A Deacon's Corner Book
Deacon's Corner Publications
Reno, Nevada

Cover Design by C. R. Lanham

Echoes of Love
Copyright © 2015, Charles R. Lanham, Deacon

All rights reserved. No part of this book may be reproduced, stored in a retrieval system, or transmitted, in any form or by any means, electronic, mechanical, photocopying, recording, or otherwise, without the prior written permission of the author.

ISBN-13: 978-0-9905582-4-8
ISBN-10: 099055824X

Published by Deacon's Corner Publications
Reno, Nevada 89519

Printed and bound in the United States of America.

Dedication

To Janet, with all my love.

Contents

What Greater Love 1

Off Angels' Wings 5

Memories 11

Searching for Camelot 21

Sunrise Dancing 41

Wanting More 49

Ode To An Angel 55

The Labyrinth 61

From Dreams Ascending 71

Rude Awakening 75

And God Knows 89

Once Upon A Memory 93

Echoes of Love 99

From A Distance 107

Of Love 117

I Believe 123

The Bonds Of Love 131

Preface

THERE is a special beauty that only manifests itself whenever a soul finds itself in the presence of a soulmate. It's a beauty that dwells below the surface, hidden deep within, until encouraged by love, it finds the desire and the courage to take wing and fly above the clouds. Beauty such as this can only bloom when nourished by forever love, which over time, is heard in whispers, memories, and echoes of love.

As someone who has known such love I am always fascinated to find others who have loved as long as or longer than I, especially those who have been soulmates for fifty, sixty, even seventy years or more. What secret do they possess to explain such longevity?

It is my sincere hope that this book, in some small way, may help you discover some of the answers, but in the final analysis the secret isn't really a secret at all. It is the willingness and desire of two souls to love the other more than life itself, to live in mutual self-sacrificing, unconditional love for the other. But exactly what does it mean to love another in such a way?

Have you ever spent any time, a few days perhaps, totally and completely surrounded and immersed in love? Now I will admit that in a sense this is a trick question, for in order to adequately and truthfully answer it one must first understand to what form of love the question is referring.

And yes, love comes in many forms, but due primarily to linguistic limitations we find it increasingly difficult to differentiate between these forms and in doing so we have diminished love to the least common denominator, to its basest form. In truth, we have made love a cheap commodity rather than a priceless heirloom. It is no small wonder that we find ourselves confused in our relationships when we have no clear understanding of what it means to love.

Consider for a moment all the things that we say we love: our spouses, our parents, our siblings, our relatives, our friends. We say we love God, baseball, and apple pie. We love our dogs, cats, trees, flowers, cars, clothes, and so much more. Obviously we cannot love all of these in the same way. We cannot love pizza in the same way as we love our parents. We may love flowers but certainly not to the same degree as we love a friend, a brother, or a sister.

Love is clearly not a "one size fits all" word, yet that is what we have made it in our everyday argot. Rather than a single word to describe all the forms of love, the Greek language has five words for love; five words that distinguish between five very different forms of love.

1. *Mania* – is the love of possession, an obsessive desire to own, even madness.
2. *Eros* – is emotional love; the feeling of love.
3. *Phileos* – is friendship; sharing common interests; fondness for things.
4. *Storge* – is love for a dependent; parental love.
5. *Agape* – is love that requires no response; seeks the best for another; charity.

Without the means to differentiate between one form of love and another we find ourselves placing all forms into a blender and pressing *puree*. What pours out is no longer a golden elixir but a nauseous combination heavily weighted to its lowest forms. The sweet delicate taste of *Agape* has been curdled and soured, overpowered by the urgencies of *Eros* and the obsessions of *Mania*. The beauty of *Agape* love has been transposed into an ugly, cheap four-letter word.

Some time ago I spent four marvelous days totally and completely surrounded, immersed in four of the five forms of love (No *Mania*.) I cannot recall ever having had such an experience but I can only hope and pray to God that he will allow me to do so again for it was marvelous and life-changing. Celebrating a granddaughter's birthday with her parents and her brother, I loved and felt love four ways and then some. Reuniting with classmates, some I had not seen for fifty years was heavy on the *Philos*, with a good measure of emotional *Eros* thrown in. Spending a few days and evenings with a dear friend was overwhelmingly the same. Offering the Eucharist to family, friends, and classmates was pure *Agape*.

God is *Agape* and he calls us to *love* others as we *love* ourselves, but we must know the difference. Forever love is God in us, it is *Agape*.

I am, I believe, first and foremost a hopeless romantic and a hopeful scribbler, someone who enjoys the challenge of expressing my thoughts in what I trust can be genuinely described as cogent and meaningful prose. For those who are familiar with my writing, you will know that my style is normally quite prosaic, which by implication generally means that it lacks any quality which might remotely be ascribed as poetic beauty.

While I have, until recently, never thought of myself as particularly creative, I have discovered that perhaps I have judged myself a bit too harshly in that regard. When I reflect on my life and my particular passions, I find a great deal more creativity there than I have ever recognized or been willing to acknowledge. Yet I will be the first to admit that whatever creativity I might possess is a talent not of my own making but a gift that comes to me solely through the grace of God, the Creator of all that is and ever shall be. And he created it all from nothing! Now that is what I call creative genius!

Although I seldom attempt to write in verse (for those who might be unfamiliar with the word, it is synonymous with poetry,) that doesn't mean that I am incapable of doing so or that I have never tried my hand at it. The very fact that this small book is in your hands is proof that I have and I do hope that you enjoy it as much as I have enjoyed writing it.

While this work contains my own poor attempts at verse, I must admit that I am not as prolific in its form as I would like to be. Thus what follows is somewhat of a hybrid work consisting of both introductory prose and verse.

In this effort I have found that each genre is decidedly different and, while both may engage the same language, each exercises linguistic gymnastics uniquely its own. Thus any attempt to find common ground among such dissimilar creative art forms presents more than a few interesting challenges. I will leave it to you to determine if it was worth the effort.

Deacon Chuck Lanham
Reno, Nevada
December 2015

Acknowledgements

LET ME first confess that for the most part I remain deeply indebted to those who helped, guided, assisted, and contributed to my previous work. While I could perhaps have omitted mention of them here I still owe them each a debt which I have little hope of ever repaying. In some small way I suppose in acknowledging them here I can repay a minute portion of that debt.

It is with the deepest devotion and gratitude that I begin by acknowledging the Source and

Creator of all things. For without God and His infinite love, all of creation – and with absolute certainty, this book – would simply not exist. I am especially grateful for His patience, forgiveness, love, and persistence in waiting for this poor broken creature to finally come to his senses.

Without the steadfast love, support, and prayers of my wife Janet, who has ever walked beside me through my self-imposed exile in the desert and the valley of death for over forty-seven years, I could never have entered the Promised Land. I can only say that you are truly a saint and I have and will always love you.

I was brought into this world through the love of my parents, Bob and Nellie Ann Lanham. They raised me, nurtured me, and loved me, but above all they gifted me with the example of what true devotion and love ought to be.

My father taught me how the poor in spirit shall see God. He taught me how to love and honor another. He taught me what it meant to always do your best while focusing on the needs of others. My mother taught me how the meek shall inherit the earth. She taught me the power and wonder of the written word and how to use it as a voice for good. Above all, they both taught me faith. They lived it, breathed it, and tried their utmost to be true examples of Christ in all that they said and did. I think of them every day and miss them terribly.

A very special group which has had a profound impact on this current work consists of my ten amazing siblings and their families. While wishing to acknowledge each individually by name, I fear doing so would far exceed the number of pages of this book so I will simply mention my siblings. As I am the first, they are in order after me: Robert, Christopher (deceased,) Geoffrey, Mary Kay, Elizabeth, Eric, Jeaniene, Nicholas, Maureen, and Karen. Each of my brothers and sisters, in their own unique way, has shown how to truly love one another and how to love others as Christ asked us to do.

God works His marvelous deeds in many ways and it is often through the lives of others that He speaks to us so clearly. My journey back to Him began when I first visited my cousin Vicki Fach and her husband Wes along with their growing family for it was an unforgettable religious experience that truly humbled and inspired me. Their faith and love has renewed my spirit and lifted my soul to God.

I continue to owe a great debt to my friend, neighbor, and spiritual director, Monique Jacobs. Her patience, forbearance, wisdom, and counsel have kept this often lost soul on the narrow path. She has also taught me how to become a passenger rather than always attempting to take the wheel away from God.

Above all I wish to thank the countless individuals through whom God has spoken to me over the years. You almost certainly do not know who you are for you were never aware of Him at the time, but I assure you, He was there and I heard His voice in you.

God bless you all.

Echoes of Love

What Greater Love

Within each moment

THERE is a moment and a story behind every poem. A poem is born with its own unique character, much like snowflakes and fingerprints; every line gravid with meaning only fully understood by the poet. In that sense a poem mirrors what lies within the soul for, as I have written elsewhere, the soul is a sanctuary where only two can dwell: the self and God, and only those who reside within can know the entirety and meaning of you. The rest of us may only guess.

Unlike prose, poetry lives in the world of dreams, filled with metaphor and symbolic imagery, leaving the reader to decide what it all means, to fill in the blanks drawing on one's own experiences and imagination.

Upon the dedication page for **The Voices of God** I penned a small poem, which at the time I gave little weight or significance but upon reflection, I now believe it to have served as a harbinger for this work, coming from where else but the Voice of God. If only I would have listened then.

There is a reason and a purpose,
within each moment that we live;
as we pass through every season
God calls us all to give
our love to all His creatures,
His creatures great and small.
Know the love of God and neighbor
is the greatest love of all.

Off Angels' Wings
Look and see the face of God

FOR MANY Americans, Thanksgiving is a pivotal moment in the steady march toward a new year, marking the onset of what is commonly called the "holiday season". Bookended by the national holiday and the ringing in of the New Year, the season is filled with a madcap rush of non-stop activities centered on family gatherings, shopping, decorating, cooking, parties, and more. The air is filled with insistent voices urging everyone to stop whatever they are doing and shop, shop, shop. Each passing day only serves to increase the sense of impending doom should one fail to get it while it lasts!

Lost in all the hype and blather is the true reason for the season and recognition that there are those who will find it impossible to participate in this festive time. With all of the activities that ensue in preparation for the Thanksgiving holiday, our thoughts are seldom focused on the why?

Each year it seems, fewer and fewer can either recall or care to consider the basis upon which we come together to celebrate any of the holidays that occur over the final days of the year. The prevalent attitude appears to be that there need be no reason for bacchanalian celebration.

Forgotten are those who find themselves in circumstances much like a poor Jewish carpenter and his very pregnant wife who found themselves in unfamiliar surroundings, friendless, alone, and homeless. Those who did not share their circumstances gave no thought to their plight as they went about their ordinary and busy lives. They traveled through the masses as if they were wrapped in invisibility cloaks. It was the darkest of times.

But there came a night, a time of new birth, when light off angels' wings dispelled the darkness and the heavens sang with joyful noise. It was a time when those who lived among the shadows received unexpected visitors whose presence lifted their spirits and brought them the gift of hope. And the visitors received the greatest gift of all for they looked upon the newborn child and saw the face of God.

As we journey through the coming days, let us take a moment to remind ourselves of the bounty and blessings which God has bestowed on us and take a moment to remember those less fortunate. And let us be the lamp that brings light to those in darkness and fire to warm the hearts of those who lay shivering in the cold.

I penned the poem that follows as I looked upon the partially snow-covered ground that lay outside my window one Thanksgiving afternoon some years ago. As I sat in comfort before a welcoming fire I realized just how blessed I was to be in a warm, safe place, filled with the satisfaction and contentment that comes from sharing a bountiful feast with family and friends. And while I sat enjoying the moment an uneasy disquietude began to slowly seep into my consciousness, disrupting my otherwise pleasant musings.

There is nothing wrong with having enough or even plenty, just so long as we recognize that there are those who have little or nothing at all, and do something, anything, to share our abundance with those who are in need. Jesus always looked with love and charity toward those who found themselves in need, recognizing that poverty will never be completely eradicated from the human condition. It is incumbent upon all who have much to help those who have little. Give thanks to God by giving what you can to others for it is in giving that you receive, it is in recognizing the stranger that you will see the face of God, and in loving the unloved that you will bring light off angels' wings to those in darkness.

Remnants of a recent snow,
ragged blankets still lay covering,
(earth now dreaming pleasant memories)
breathe cold and whispered vapors
that waft upon the silent, bracing breeze,
and speak of life beyond the dead of winter.

The fire that burns within, repels
the uninvited grip of winter's death;
and darkness demands unwelcome audience
with the Light which by its nature does deny
entrance to the shadows that are want to fill
the soul with dread and raw despair.

Spirits dance among the embers,
echoes of once twinkling laughter,
reflections of lives joined together,
loomed with thread so tightly woven,
measured bonds from lamps undimmed,
bent in gratitude for gifts bestowed.

Ghosts of what well might have been,
resurrected tales of deeds profound,
sins long denied and unremembered
add substance with such fond affection
to the gilded idol, admired and savored,
consumed in sacrifice to the grateful bowed.

The bell that tolls with every hour
marks the unrelenting beat that tramples
through long forgot, forsaken tenements
where denizens reside in hopeless squalor
pummeled by the frigid force of winter's breath
that blows through open sores of lost regret.

The flickering light off angels' wings
purchase what flames in darkness prove:
dark a barren handmaid, light its master.
Rare do angels tread upon dark and ebon shores
yet know the smallest light shone fully
upon a stranger will illumine no other than

       the Face of God.

Memories

Of a love now gone

LIFE is a precious gift on lease to us by God which owns but the briefest presence among the living. Neither its beginning nor its ending is within our power to determine or control. It is the living of it that lingers beyond its ending, which brings long forgotten memories to the fore. We can but hope that all which will be remembered of us will bring full measure of a life well-lived for above all else we wish to be remembered well.

Maya Anjelou once wrote, *"I've learned that people will forget what you said, people will forget what you did, but people will never forget how you made them feel"* and there is great truth in what she wrote. We each have our own journey to travel, some walk along but the shortest path, while others find their way home only after many tortuous and difficult miles. Ralph Waldo Emerson opined that *"Life is a journey, not a destination"* and that is equally true, but I would offer that a journey without a destination lays waste to the life of any traveler. Wandering aimlessly serves no purpose and ultimately gets you nowhere.

It is neither our words nor our deeds but the poverty of spirit that inscribes the memories upon which we will be remembered. Neither wealth nor fame will bear witness beyond the grave. What will be remembered long after journey's end may well be but this brief epitaph: *"When asked to give, all was given."*

Jesus said *"Blessed are the poor in spirit, for theirs is the kingdom of heaven"*[1] and we most often take this to include those who are without wealth or other worldly goods. But Jesus was

---

[1] Mt 5:3.

admonishing all of us, regardless of our station in life that it was to those who gave all that they could to help others, to those who impoverished their own spirit in order to nourish and provide for those in greater need who would be given the keys to the kingdom of heaven.

We should remind ourselves often of what God told his people through the prophet Isaiah, "*…my thoughts are not your thoughts, nor are your ways my ways,…*"[2] for truly we have no way of knowing what he has in store for us. Consider how often we, through happy circumstance, encounter a soul somewhere along the way who fills an emptiness that lies within us, lifts our spirit, shares a burden, or brings new life into the world?

I have met death many times in my life and this I have learned from those encounters: the loss will be the worst of it and the missing will be indelibly etched upon your hearts but know as well that joy and fond remembrance will

---

[2] Is 55:8.

endure long beyond the immediacy of the pain and sorrow.

Yet no matter how many times death precedes you, each encounter leaves an indelible mark upon your soul, an anguished pit which once held loving memories now gone.

Rare are the souls we encounter who have a profound and lasting effect upon everyone they meet. Even rarer are those who unknowingly and without recompense have significantly and positively made a difference in the lives of so many even those of whom they have never met.

I have been blessed to have known several such souls who made a difference by their presence and their marvelous and giving hearts.

I will speak here of my brother Chris, who was one of those remarkable souls. What remains are but memories of him and yet they are memories that make us feel good, memories that warm the heart and fill the soul, reminders of his constant love and infectious laughter.

With Chris you often either wanted to kiss him, hug him, slap him or slug him; and on occasion all at the same time. He was a legend, both to those who knew him, and in his own mind. He was always ready and eager to regale you with a tale or two…or three…or four…and it made no difference whether you had heard them before (and most who knew him had heard them over and over again) yet Chris never let that stop him from retelling them once more. He was the consummate people person, regularly calling, stopping by, visiting, or simply staying in touch with those he had come to know, and there were so many whose lives he had touched throughout the years.

Yet, above all else, Chris exemplified more than most what Jesus meant when he called us to be poor in spirit, for he gave all that he had to give. Stories abound of his generosity, from those who he offered his home without reservation or hesitation, of money lent or simply given to those in greater need, of a helping hand to those who simply asked, of his fierce loyalty and steadfast devotion to his family and many friends. But above all else, it was his love and friendship so enthusiastically and freely given to everyone he met that will be best remembered.

Chris was not perfect, far from it, but he was always "poor in spirit" and for all that he so freely gave, never asking or expecting anything in return, his is the kingdom of heaven.

Without him life marches on as it does with any passing, but life remains the better for his living of it. He remains within our hearts and minds, if not in body but in spirit and always in our memories.

I spoke these words in eulogy at my brother's funeral. In preparing it, many other thoughts — fond memories really — welled up from deep inside and I felt compelled to write the elegy that follows.

In addition to my love for writing prose and verse, I must confess that I have also tried my hand at music composition. In the wake of Chris's death I heard a melody from deep inside my heart and, while it took some time, I have managed to put it to paper, a composition in the form of a piano sonata which I call **Reflections on a Memory**.

The pain of his passing has been tempered by time but every time I read this elegy or play that music, I am reminded of just how much I miss him and of his incredible love for his family, friends, life, and his God.

*Oh! Thy effervescent memories
that echo yet down silent halls
and fill the wind with lingering breath
which once gave such sweet laughter
mention to the clamoring throng.*

*Music felled the raging storm
and song dispelled the darkened sky
giving flight to untried wings.
And love did tame the fires of hell
and quenched the anguish of the damned.*

*Pain and sorrow took a bow
bending to thy unyielding spirit
that dared to laugh at every aching
while yet more life was left to live
as life itself had more to offer.*

*Burdens carried with no quarrel
Strangers lost, long discarded.
Friends forever well remembered
beyond the edge of distant memory
steeled with much requited love.*

*Ghosts of distant daring deeds
wafting aimlessly among the weeds
and embellished tales of yesteryear
retold as though the first in telling
of oft told tales so familiar.*

*Oh sweet laughter, twinkling eye!
You graced us with your living large
and held us fast with bonds so strong
as if thy will alone would be enough
to last for all eternity.*

*Such memories that must remain
are poor imposters, nothing more,
reflections on a darkened mirror
that stand beyond what once had been
and forever shall be never more.*

*Thy spirit does invade the senses
with whispers, soft and gently smiling
what hold no hint of pain or sorrow,
no regrets for the parting
only joy forever after.*

*The missing is what scars the soul
and stabs the heart with brittle pain
leaving nothing but the absence
of the steady beat of time expected,
knowing that it beats no more.*

*The ear in anticipation listens
for the tolling of the bell,
for the door again to open,
for the ungainly step to fall
yet knowing it will never happen,
not again, no never more.*

Searching for Camelot

It never rains after sundown

THERE is a familiar epigram attributed to Jean-Baptiste Alphonse Karr of which he penned, *"plus ça change, plus c'est la même chose"* usually translated as *"the more things change, the more they stay the same."* While in all likelihood not Karr's intended meaning, this somehow seems apropos as a metaphor for much of life.

Each and every life begins and ends much the same way: there is a moment when life comes into being, while quite clearly the instant before it did not; likewise, there comes a moment when life exists and in the next instant it is not.

What happens between the beginning and the end is never quite the same, is it? Every life has its own unique path upon which it travels; some paths are short while others would appear to go on forever.

Count the seconds between the beginning and the ending and each will vary, never lasting exactly for the same amount of time. Some paths appear straight and level while most are strangely bent and tortured by hardships and obstacles met along the way.

But as much as each and every journey differs from all others, there is much that remains the same for we are each created by God in his image and likeness and it is our humanity in which we all share a common bond.

Every one of us experiences life and faces the challenges set before us in stages. Each of us meets those challenges in our own way. Some may find what life presents to be too difficult or too great a challenge and thus refuse to continue profitably on their journey. We find far too many of these unfortunate souls who have lost their way and the will to overcome obstacles set before them, residing in doorways, street corners, and alleyways.

For those remaining, we accept the difficulties and hardships that arise along the way with determination, spirit, and courage. We live out our lives loving God, our neighbors, and ourselves. Some find *forever love*, united in love with a soul so sublime as to be nearly divine.

> "If we had no winter,
> the spring would not be so pleasant;
> if we did not sometimes taste of adversity,
> prosperity would not be so welcome."
>
> Anne Bradstreet 1612-16-72

Our lives can be observed through the prism of the seasons and while the seasons may vary in their intensity and duration, most of us will find ourselves experiencing each season much as everyone else while living each quite differently.

Spring

Winter's breath, with sharp regret, blows
o'er barren fields where long ago
new life sprang from a fertile womb
unblemished yet by troubles met,
nor tarnished by the stain of sin,
kept safe in humor's loving arms
while nurtured at a mother's breast
and gently bathed with tears of joy,
caressed to sleep with lullabies
sung soft and low, at peaceful rest.

Softly now, with a tender touch,
winter's breath slowly turns to spring,
young lives unfurl gossamer wings
reluctant to embrace the sky
lest the sun should deny them space
to soar unfettered where they would
undaunted by what lay beyond,
innocence unspoiled by the wounds
of consequence and misspent youth,
eager to confront new each day.

*Fresh breezes waft among the clouds
while gentle showers do provide
release for those poor captive souls
burdened by bonds of such sweet love
which does reprove of letting those
with wings so young to fly alone
above the clouds and out of reach
of what boundless love would protect,
beyond all care or thought of self
no price too great, all pain endured.*

*The sound of laughter fills the air
with such sweet carefree melody
performed in perfect harmony
without discord or somber note
to mar the joyful music played
with exuberant abandon
by those too young to care or know
what will be found at rainbow's end,
no matter what the fables say,
a city paved with streets of gold.*

*Who once did rest at mother's breast
calmed by the beating of her heart,
comforted by her gentle touch,
and safely held in loving arms
often tired beyond all caring,
now has begun to pull away
from the love so freely given,
to break familiar bonds of love
without regard for pain or loss,
so helpless once, now want to fly.*

*Oh sweet spring, sweet impatient spring
you leave us wanting; begging you
to linger well beyond the days
which fortune has allotted you.
It is not you we would detain
for summer eagerly awaits,
rather tis those who would demur
from leaving Neverland in haste
lest the laughter be forgotten,
mere unremembered memories.*

Summer's coming; it will not wait
for spring to tarry anymore.
Ingénues prance with poise and grace,
with eyes that stare upon the prize
which they would eagerly devour
without mercy, without remorse
to stand upon the pedestal
and claim their rightful place above
the common throng who would adore
this golden idol all the more.

Spring's acolytes have dimmed the lights
and closed the curtains on their play
to sleep awhile, perhaps to dream
of roses and of daffodils,
of gentle breezes, soft and warm,
and clouds and rain and growing things.
Untried wings anticipate,
undaunted by what lies beyond
for all they understand is now,
before them stands eternity.

Summer

With heavy heart spring bids adieu
and brushes summer's golden hair
as she blithely laughs and dances
leaving summer with her charges,
now rid the chains which did restrain
what with imagination wild
did conceive of wanton pleasures
which heretofore had been denied
for the sanctity of the soul
and the purity of the heart.

The summer sun struts with conceit,
flattered by praise best undeserved,
yet holding firm to the belief
that all revolves around the king.
The children laughed and pranced about
no thoughts of what may lay ahead,
while once upon a sunbeam bright,
the children played with abandon,
never caring for tomorrow,
nothing mattered except the play.

*All the children adored the sun
and reveled in all its glory,
believing its impassioned heat
displayed true love with perfection,
without thought or recognition
simply caring for the feeling
of passion's breath and in wanting
for a moment love imagined
to exist beyond the purest
act of unblemished sanctity.*

*The young enamored by the sun
believe they know more than they do,
and care not whether what they know
is truly truth or fairy tale.
Important things, they do believe,
can be discovered in a book
which they will never for themselves
read much beyond the cover page
for vanity demands they take
a break; besotted foolishness.*

*Journeys never fly straight and true,
nor is the destination known.
The road, so rare paved flat and smooth,
stretched well beyond horizon's edge,
what unknown miles before the end
must be trod with stalwart heart,
unbridled spirit, courage too
to reach beyond what might have been,
to climb the highest mountain peak,
to grasp the stars with calloused hands.*

*Those who dare fly beyond the sun
are those who would with courage greet
the summer sun with but a nod
and turn aside from lesser things
to ride the tempest with disdain,
to soar to heights beyond the sky,
and look upon dark abyssal depths
for such purpose but of knowing
what has never been discovered,
to touch and see what God has made.*

*Love enters with an emptiness
and catches but a brief report
of another soul so yearning
for much more than passing passion,
needing more than most will offer,
wanting what would last forever,
longing for a flame eternal
which would form a perfect union,
souls together for evermore
impassioned by the bonds of love.*

*With the passing days of summer
burning with unbridled fury
on mortal souls who dare defy
the raging madness of the sun
seeking shelter among the trees
where breezes temper summer's heat,
to drink refreshing lemonade
from frosty glasses, icy cold,
laughing at the sun's frustration;
time is passing, summer's ending.*

Autumn

Those who would remain in summer,
they will quickly be forgotten,
discarded souls among the weeds,
slowly dying from their neglect,
their foolishness has aged them so,
beyond redemption, lost forever
in hopeless squalor and despair,
insistently demanding more
from those who have what they have not,
insisting that it's not their fault.

The green of summer changes hue
as autumn steps upon the stage
dismissing summer with her smile
and slowly calms the antic pace
while unfolding all the beauty
which God has lovingly bestowed,
a gift to mark the beginning
of the season painted golden,
when the living give thanks to God
for all the blessings they've received.

Looking back upon seasons past
autumn smiles with satisfaction
at what began so long ago,
of her children in summer now,
while their children in spring now play.
The journey is yet full complete,
for there are many miles to go,
some memories are bittersweet
recalling what might well have been
and what was never meant to be.

The days grow short, are cooler now,
still the wood displays her splendor
dyed rich with yellow, red, and gold.
Seed sown in spring in furrowed rows
has grown, matured, and prospered well.
Forest creatures prepare their beds
and fill their larder well and full
knowing what with speed approaches
after autumn's time has ended,
winter's frigid death comes knocking.

*What voices raised so stridently
above the roar of summer play
no longer stand on center stage
to spew unthinking diatribes
full force upon the crowd below.
The third act plays an interlude
filled with peace and quietude
and warm aromas in the air
whisper among the evergreens
inviting all who linger there.*

*Wistful memories of regret
in whispered voices soft and low
tease the wind across the meadow,
still waters ripple o'er the pond
shivering from a sudden chill,
the aching soul in contemplation
reflects upon what disappoints,
at what was lost or left undone,
for unforgiven sins: remorse,
knowing winter fast approaches.*

As falling leaves spread their blanket
over carpet worn thin and bare
by the passage of the seasons
and all who played among the trees,
fleeting shadows begin to kiss
the edges of the forest keep
and the stones standing row on row
reminders of another time
when lovers hand in hand would walk
and laugh at nothing much at all.

Autumn's smile is now the softer,
turned as much as Whistler's mother.
What once was openly enjoyed,
treasured beyond all measure,
with avarice and greed obtained,
no longer shines with the luster
which did entice and overwhelm
the heart and mind and the senses.
Wisdom often arrives well late
yet far better late than never.

*Vestigial leaves on naked trees
testify with grave reluctance
to the unrelenting ticking,
the measured beating of the clock
which in accordance to the law
bears witness to the sentinel
who stands before the throne of God
to determine who shall enter,
to walk upon streets paved with gold
forever and forever more.*

Winter

*Among the throng some do enjoy
what bitter temper winter sends,
reveling in the frigid air,
racing down steep mountain traces,
sliding over frozen waters
while laughing at her philippic
and taunting her with such disdain
in hopes her fury will increase
well beyond mortal boundaries
creating a perfect playground.*

Winter brings a quiet stillness,
those in slumber dream of summer
safely hidden from winter's rage
and her dark dystopian funk,
a harbinger of what awaits
those who would offend the silence
by denying death an entrance,
laughing at its dark demeanor
while dancing o'er a vacant grave
to the tune of Summertime.

For most, what winter does portend,
is seldom welcomed with desire,
for what was once filled with laughter
stands now shuttered against the cold
and what embers left are dimming,
casting shadows across the room
while puppets dance upon the wall
to entertain without a sound
those who now in silence keeping
mourn the missing of love now gone.

A cold chill wind invades within,
thru locked doors and shuttered windows;
death can never long be denied
for no one can escape the toll
which must be paid at journey's end;
without exception all will pay
and the price will be determined
by the love that was extended
to a neighbor, friend, or stranger
requiring nothing in return.

The final quarter does provide
small comfort for the traveler
seeking shelter against the wind.
To sit before a hearty fire
and feel the warmth a moment more,
while holding close the memories
of yesterday and long ago,
when the horizon stood afar
well beyond imagination
believing it would never end.

Forever love will never fail,
tho' tempests blow with much avail
and mile on mile may separate;
no storm or hardship can prevail
against what God has thus united.
Mortality, you can never
extinguish the flame yet burning
deep within one heart still beating
and the soul of one no longer
bound by earthly limitations.

Ever should death's unwelcome hand
catch a traveler by surprise,
it should be said at journey's end,
whenever that should come to pass,
that the traveler wintered well
without regrets or sorrow too
but rather smiled at the prospect
of new adventures that await,
no more winters, only summers
so mild and warm, like Camelot.

Sunrise Dancing

Soaring high above the stage

HAVE you ever watched a sunrise and listened to the music of the dawn played by nature's orchestra and chorus, a grand symphonic performance now playing just beyond your bedroom window?

The song sung by the mountain quail and mourning dove so soft and low in the gentle morning breeze that whispers as the sun peeks beyond the mountains to the east. The breath of air that combs your hair and cools your face as it softly lulls you back to sleep.

Such moments are all too often left for the young to enjoy; for those who have moved beyond the unencumbered years of youthful exuberance and careless freedom find little time to waste on such idleness. And that is truly sad for we miss so much of life as we go about the daily act of living.

Each of us should take note that when the sun has dipped below the horizon and the daylight slowly fades away, the night sings a dirge to its passing and we, in slumber, mimic death. Christ's death and resurrection are thus reenacted to remind us, with each and every revolution of our planet that for life to begin anew it first must always meet with death.

As Jesus has told us, *"unless a grain of wheat falls to the ground and dies, it remains just a grain of wheat; but if it dies, it produces much fruit. Whoever loves his life loses it, and whoever hates his life in this world will preserve it for eternal life."*[3] There will always be those who believe in only now, who wish to remain a grain a wheat, who

---

[3] Jn 12:24-25.

love their life as it is above all else and refuse to look beyond this moment, this now. How sad it is when the caterpillar denies the butterfly its wings.

With each new day a resurrection, we should bend a knee to the One who gave us life and beauty, music and dancing, love and laughter. Live the moment as when you were young and carefree. Feel and breathe in the dawning of a new day. Take in the rising of the Son and bask in the blessings and glory of Almighty God.

*The sweet breath of summer whispers
soft and low thru meadow grass
and sunrise still at slumber's rest
begins to stir from pleasant dreams
to waken to a dawning sky.*

*Still and silent then the music,
which did play with such abandon
when evening shadows dimmed the light
and with the night did murmur soft
until it slept and sang no more.*

*Bright dancers wink on ebon sky
then bow with such amazing grace
and with sad reluctance bid adieu
vowing to reprise their play
when the sun gives way to night.*

*The sleepers stir within their beds
and gently rub the night away
and slowly lift their heads to sing
their rising song to call the sun
to dance anew upon the sky.*

With anticipation building,
night's ink fades slowly into gray,
and the sun kisses night farewell;
the tempo of the music moves
from gravé to allegretto.

The dance begins with little mention
as the sun peeks o'er the rim
revealing angels fast asleep
buried deep beneath their blankets
of floating iridescent mist.

Rising, rising, ever rising
on its inexorable dance
the sun soars high above the stage
and shimmering visions do appear
which give the sun its royal glow.

Starlight dancers have left the stage,
waiting patiently in the wings
while the sun performs ballet
with perfect form leaps grand jeté
on its quotidian round.

Gossamer wings of butterflies
float aimlessly on morning's breath
while hummingbirds sip sweet nectar
from bright flowers smiling skyward
swaying absently in the breeze.

The mourning dove and mountain quail
tiptoe across narrow fences
murmuring softly to their mates
of nothing much, and then they pause
to admire the dawn's performance.

White cotton floats on denim sky,
soft pillows for angelic wings
to sit and ponder and to wonder
what pleasantries the day may bring
and to watch God's works at play.

The burbling brook sings lullabies
to those who come to drink from it
and lay beneath the stately trees
enchanted by the passing sun
that winks at them as it dances.

High above the stage he rises
and the earth sings Hallelujah
as the star attains its zenith
far above the throng adoring,
basking in reflected glory.

The crowd calls for intermission,
a brief respite to catch their breath
beneath the shaded mezzanine
where gentle breezes whisper soft
lulling the audience to sleep.

While they doze the dance continues
for never does the sun delay
what has with precision crafted
been choreographed by our God
for no other could do so well.

As the performance approaches
the western exit of the stage
the sun begins its final dance
the grand denouement to the day
while the crowd demands an encore.

*Alas, the sun declines to stay
for the dance has proved exhausting
which quickly finds the star asleep
no doubt dreaming of tomorrow
when another dance is scheduled.*

*Reclining in its feather bed
the sun now turns the lights down low
leaving the stage to the nighttime
and the evening orchestra
prepares to play its nightly song.*

Wanting More

It is enough to know we love

LOVE is often complicated, messy, and poorly understood by those who believe they are masters of it. What is often taken to be love is seldom love at all but rather infatuation or a desire for intimacy coupled with passion. We live in an age where casual hookups and one-night stands have replaced intentional long-lasting relationships built upon authentic mutual self-giving love.

I have long believed that love has best been described – in near perfect verse – by Saint Paul in First Corinthians:

> *Love is patient,*
> *love is kind.*
>
> *It is not jealous,*
> *love is not pompous,*
> *it is not inflated,*
> *it is not rude,*
> *it does not seek its own interest,*
> *it is not quick-tempered,*
> *it does not brood over injury,*
> *it does not rejoice over wrongdoing*
> *but rejoices with the truth.*
>
> *It bears all things,*
> *believes all things,*
> *hopes all things,*
> *endures all things.*
>
> *Love never fails."*[4]

One thing I have learned after nearly one-half century of being in love with my love is that love must be nourished and sustained for it to endure for a lifetime. You must provide the food to feed your love and that requires a lot of

---

[4] 1 Cor 13:4-8.

hard work and devoted energy. Love is never easy nor is it free or cheaply purchased for you indeed get what you pay for, yet forever love is priceless and worth everything.

In order to love one another you must first like one another, respect one another, be proud of one another. It is crucial that you remember those things that attracted you to each other and hold onto to those when times get tough — and there *will* be tough times.

For myself, I have always been inordinately proud of my wife who I know is much smarter than I and far more capable. She is simply irreplaceable to me, as I firmly trust I am to her. It is our love that became one so many years ago and it is our love that binds us still.

You have to feel that same way about each other. In a very real sense when you marry, you lose yourself and become one body, one spirit. Just as parts of your bodies are irreplaceable, so must you be to each other. Take care of that which is irreplaceable and your love will be well-fed and complete.

No one should interpret what I have just said as a proclamation of a perfect and saccharine relationship borne without occasional strife, discord, or hardships for that would simply not be the case.

Many years ago prior to my own wedding my mother offered me sage advice, advice which I have never forgotten and have always tried to honor. She told me that marriage is not a 50/50 proposition—it is a 150/150 proposition. You must always be willing to give more than you ever expect to receive. And in giving more you will receive more.

Support one another, accept one another's faults and failures as your own, and live together as one body with and for the honor and glory of God. Keep God close to you, make Him an essential part of your life together, and He will bless you with an abundance of gifts of love and happiness for the rest of your lives.

*Oh how we once did soar with grace
to lofty heights above the clouds,
and we did fly too near the sun
and thus our hearts did melt
from the torrid heat of our desire
while our descent from heaven's gate
left us wanting, wanting more.*

*Once upon a time, so long ago,
across a crowded room we met,
and talked and talked and talked
and talked of many things, and yet,
we could not fill our souls with knowing
all that was the other, for it merely
left us wanting, wanting more.*

*The days of yesterday have slipped away
all but forgotten among the boxes
filled with "what might have been-s"
and "what was never meant to be-s".
But there were moments, oh such moments
when joyous gifts thrice surprised and
left us wanting, wanting more.*

*Do you ponder as I wonder
when the knowing of the other
was enough to simply be
in quiet presence, nothing more?
When did we soar beyond the sun
into cathedral silence, knowing nothing
left us wanting, wanting more?*

*It does not matter why or wherefore,
it is enough to know we love
the other more beyond the telling,
beyond the heat of passion's breath,
beyond the knowing of the other.
It is enough to love, my love,
forever wanting, wanting more.*

*Love whispers soft and low such
sweet music from the heart and
every note and measured beat
sings with such perfect harmony
a melody so pure the soul cries out
in sublime and joyful agony
echoes of love, wanting more.*

Ode To An Angel

I gave my heart away

GREAT musical productions which contain such marvelous songs are precious gifts which we are want to breathe in deep and allow them to carry us away. Perhaps my favorite musical and film has always been South Pacific[5] and from it such song as *Some Enchanted Evening*, *Younger Than Springtime*, *Bali Ha'i*, and *This Nearly Was Mine* were memorized and sung often, loudly, and

---

[5] Joshua Logan, Richard Rogers, Oscar Hammerstein II, *South Pacific*, 1949 Broadway musicial, 1958 film, based on James A. Michener's 1947 book, *Tales of the South Pacific*.

with great feeling. But my favorite was and still remains *Some Enchanted Evening*. For me the lyrics came true when I saw a stranger across a crowded room.

Some enchanted evening
You may see a stranger,
you may see a stranger
Across a crowded room
And somehow you know,
You know even then
That somewhere you'll see her
Again and again.

Some enchanted evening
Someone may be laughing,
You may hear her laughing
Across a crowded room
And night after night,
As strange as it seems
The sound of her laughter
Will sing in your dreams.

Who can explain it?
Who can tell you why?

Fools give you reasons,
Wise men never try.

Some enchanted evening
When you find your true love,
When you feel her call you
Across a crowded room,
Then fly to her side,
And make her your own
Or all through your life you
May dream all alone.

Once you have found her,
Never let her go.
Once you have found her,
Never let her go!

I first met that stranger at a party and quite literally saw her across a crowded room and I knew then that I would see her again and again. And for nearly fifty years now the sound of her laughter still sings in my dreams. And I have no intention of ever letting her go!

*Once I saw an angel
her hair so fine and fair
it flowed with gentle curves
and billowed in the air.*

*The smile upon her lips,
melted my cares away
blinded by her beauty
I hoped that she would stay.*

*The twinkle in her eyes,
the wonder of her face
it mesmerized my soul
with such amazing grace.*

*I gave my heart away
it was all I had to give
and I hoped it would be
enough for we to live.*

*She filled my heart with love
as only angels might
she lifted my spirit
as my poor soul took flight.*

*When you see an angel
no matter when or where
know God sent her to you
for you to love and care.*

*Never harm an angel
for fragile they must be
to touch the hardened heart
with love eternally.*

*An angel is a gift
for you from God above,
to cherish more than life,
embracing you with love.*

The Labyrinth

Random thoughts of God

IT had been a long time coming but I finally decided to take the plunge and silence myself for an extended period of time. Thus I began a week-long directed silent retreat. Friends had warned that it would be a difficult experience, especially the *silent* part, so I entered the retreat center with no small amount of trepidation.

After all I really had no idea what to expect or how I would be able to occupy my days and nights sans conversation and personal interaction. But there really was nothing for me to be concerned as I learned after the first day.

In fact, at the end of day one, I felt as if I should kick myself for waiting so long.

The purpose which had driven me to the retreat was a mystery, I only knew God was behind it, compelling me to step away for a while and spend some quality time in conversation with him. I knew that I had been struggling to make any progress on what I had intended to be my second book; no matter how hard I tried I simply could not find the words or the desire to begin.

But God knew and he quite blatantly let me know on the very first day of the retreat, not once but twice, the reason for my disability and what he thought of it. The first time he spoke to me that day set the stage for the second.

At the end of each day I would write in my journal those thoughts that came to me during the day. My first day I wrote:

> What a gift today has been. I was asked by my Spiritual Director to describe how the retreat was going for me so far and I

could only describe it as *luscious*! Doesn't that sound odd? Yet, that is what it feels and tastes like, sort of like the lyrics *"Taste and see the goodness of the Lord"*.

At Morning Prayer, the reading was 1 Kings 19:11-13 which is the reading that inspired me to write my book **The Voices Of God** and which coincidently serves as the lead-in to chapter four of the aforementioned book. I could only look toward heaven and smile. He really knows how to garner your attention!

After breakfast I went for a walk and strolled through the labyrinth they have here. While I was traversing it a simple thought came to me and I started repeating (silently of course) over and over this mantra *"Puzzles amuse me, mysteries intrigue me, and questions pursue me."*

I'm not quite sure where that came from – other than from God, of course – but it stuck with me and when I returned to my room I felt compelled to pen the following poem.

It's a bit different but then it did come from God's mouth to my feeble brain so …

At Mass the evening of that first day, God prodded me a second time and it was indeed a wakeup call. Anyone who might contend that God never speaks is simply not listening.

A few years ago I was diagnosed with a serious health issue that called for major surgery. While I was told that I had a good heart some of my plumbing urgently needed major repair. This would require splitting me open, making me mostly dead by stopping my heart, replacing a portion of my aorta with a piece of garden hose, and then attempting to restart my engine with an ignition system that had only been used once, and that was more than sixty-five years prior.

To say that I was a wee bit nervous would be an understatement. A few weeks before my scheduled surgery after a restless and sleepless night filled with cold sweats and panic attacks I presided at an early morning communion service. It was difficult for me to focus on the service until at the responsorial psalm we responded *"In God I trust…"*[6] Upon hearing and saying those words all my anxiety and fears immediately and completely left me. I realized at that moment that God had a plan for me and that I was not in control. He was and He is.

I was in that instant and continue to remain at peace knowing that He has been and always will be with me, beside me, around me, and within me. I realized that He had waited patiently for me to listen to His call and to "*répondez s'il vous plaît*" and that He had much more in store for me to do. I felt so very blessed by His love and the love of those around me and I discovered perhaps later than most that that is more than enough.

Now imagine my shock and surprise when I heard that same refrain at evening Mass that

---

[6] Ps 56:11.

first day of my retreat! Once again God was beside me, telling me to be not afraid. I realized then that it was fear keeping me from writing, fear of not being up to the task, of not knowing enough, not being good enough, but most importantly, of not placing my trust in him… enough.

While I eventually set that work aside for a while, during the remaining days of the retreat I found myself writing at a frantic pace, pounding out over twelve-thousand words in a few days. I know that with God's help that book is merely at rest and that in due and proper course it will be written. In the meantime, I have found peace and great joy in this current effort.

Encountering a path so narrow,
which a traveler finds engaging
in a game of hide and seek
with those who dare to peek
beyond its long and winding way,
random thoughts of God arise.

Puzzles amuse me,
   mysteries intrigue me,
      and questions pursue me.

Mantric thoughts so softly creep,
unbidden yet with such insistence,
while walking the narrow halls
of the labyrinth forged by God.
Step softly now, tread with care
God is near, so very near.

Life astounds me,
   love gifts me,
      and God loves me.

Enter through the narrow gate
knowing not what will surprise,
knowing not the destination
knowing only that the journey
must be traveled 'til the end.
God knows its ending, only God.

Sorrow leaves me,
  joy hugs me,
    and peace calms me.

Will I wake on the morrow?
Will I see beyond the turn?
Will I travel the full measure?
Will I see the setting sun
at the ending of the day?
God knows but He's not telling.

God's in me,
  God's beside me,
    and God's with me.

With every turn encountered,
with every way addressed,
with every step advanced,
with every heartbeat measured,
with every thought possessed
thank You for loving me enough.

God heal me,
 God touch me,
  God hear me.

Looking down from celestial skies
upon the labyrinthine paths below,
the road of life lies bare and naked
of all that would surprise the traveler,
but none can scale the heights of heaven
to know what only God bestows.

God cleanse me,
 God forgive me,
  God save me.

*Soft whispered songs from angel's wings
play music for the worn and weary,
their voices kiss the wounded heart,
soothe the mind of troubled thought,
and cleanse the soul of weighty things
so you can rest within God's arms.*

From Dreams Ascending

The dreamer awakens

I NEVER KNOW where the muse will take me when I write, whether prose or verse, but I have learned to take a deep breath, empty myself of all that distracts, and allow the Holy Spirit to guide me wherever he desires for me to go.

As I have aged I have increasingly recognized that while I remain (as much as I always have) a willing and eager early sleeper, I have become a rather reluctant riser. For it would appear to me that our better dreams develop in the final moments of our slumber and like Hamlet, I cannot help but think, *"To sleep, perchance to dream—ay, there's the rub."*[7] And in truth I most often enjoy my dreams.

Often during my dreams I will have a terrific thought, so much so that I find myself instantly awake and reaching for my notepad that rests upon my nightstand to jot down what thought has caused me to wake.

It was just such a night and such a dream that woke me to the following verse.

---

[7] William Shakespeare, *Hamlet (III, i, 65-68)*.

Dreamer,
from your dreams ascending,
stirred by the winking rays
of morning sunbeams peeking
thru leaves so gently kissed
by soft whispering breeze.

Sleeper,
from your slumber waking,
yet held by images
and evanescent spirits,
who with sweet compulsion
reproves the dawning day.

Visions,
transient illusions,
flickering images
appearing in black and white,
translucent nightly ghosts
who cannot claim the day.

Darkness,
whose cloak wraps visions well
while mortal faults lie deep
beyond the veil of night
unseen by those who dwell
beyond the ebon gloom.

Sunlight,
shadows repair away
when eyes can see what they
do try so hard to hide.
The dreamer awakens
no more to sleep or dream.

Rude Awakening
From peaceful slumber

NOTICEABLY ABSENT these days from public discourse, social commentary, or didactic pedagogy is an awareness of and recognition for the essentiality of a strong moral code. Morality is a topic studiously avoided for the simple reason that any discussion of it necessarily raises uncomfortable questions and inconvenient challenges to many of our social norms, behavioral modalities, and perceptions of reality.

We are no longer guided by principles of right or wrong, good or evil but rather by our basest desires and our *"feelings"*, what feels good, or what is our *"right."* We have managed to remove *"sin"* and *"immorality"* from our lexicon; we have become amoralists, living only for ourselves and our own interests, nothing more.

Even those who most earnestly desire to live a *"moral"* life, a good life, have on too many occasions succumbed to the enticements that are laid before them. The secular, relativist vacuum which has managed to suck every mote of morality from our consciousness is principally to blame for the high level of moral decay in which we find ourselves mired. But each of us also shares in the increasing rot and decay in which we now wallow for all too quickly and easily we find ourselves closing the door on our consciences whenever we find it convenient to do so.

The problem is largely one of coating ourselves with Vaseline so that we can slide past hard moral choices without suffering pangs of guilt or shame, without remorse. Instead of choosing what we know to be objectively and morally good, we rationalize the evil that we do by degree: it's just a little white lie; it's ok to steal food if you are really hungry; it's not really a human being.

Intrinsic evil is by definition naturally evil because the act itself is absolutely contrary to reason, to nature, and to God. Such evil can never be considered good for it is not the opposite of good but rather the absence of good.

Because good cannot be both good and the absence of good (or evil,) an evil act can never be considered a good act. For instance, a truth by its nature is true and thus is good while a lie by its nature is false, as the intent is to deceive or hide the truth and thus is intrinsically evil because it is intrinsically untrue and deceptive.

Popes have written numerous encyclicals concerning intrinsic evil:

"But no reason, however grave, may be put forward by which anything intrinsically against nature may become conformable to nature and

morally good...No difficulty can arise that justifies the putting aside of the law of God which forbids all acts intrinsically evil."[8]

"...it is never lawful, even for the gravest reasons, to do evil that good may come of it — in other words, to intend directly something which of its very nature contradicts the moral order, and which must therefore be judged unworthy of man, even though the intention is to protect or promote the welfare of an individual, of a family or of society in general."[9]

Not to place too fine a point on the increasing decline in moral values, let's examine just one aspect, the matter of choice. Every human being is born with the innate ability to choose (what is commonly called *free will*) and indeed we make choices every moment of every day of our lives. Even under the most restrictive of circumstances we are free to make choices, however difficult, distasteful, horrifying, or unpleasant the choices may be. We simply

---

[8] Pope Pius XI, *Casti Cannubii*.
[9] Pope Paul VI, *Humane Vitae*, 14.

cannot avoid making choices, at least as long as we still breathe air.

Most will recognize and accept the inevitability and necessity in making choices. Far fewer are willing to acknowledge and accept that for every choice we make there are consequences, consequences which can neither be dismissed nor abrogated simply because they are inconvenient, unwanted or counter to one's desires.

To demand a "do over," that is to say, to demand the right to choose to avoid or to eliminate the consequences of a prior choice would be the height of hubris and the epitome of chutzpah. It would also be equally irresponsible and immoral.

Should a person's first choice be an immoral one, any attempt to avoid the consequences of such a choice would only serve to compound the immorality of the first. It is precisely the principle underlying the idiom *"two wrongs don't make a right."*

Without stepping too deeply into the morass euphemistically salved as *'pro-choice'* let us focus our attention on a choice seldom considered, a choice that is rooted in the immorality so prevalent today, choosing sexual intercourse, not out of love or for procreation but for the mere pleasure in doing so. The consequences of indulging in such hedonistic delights are evident in the genocidal numbers of elective abortions performed every single day.

No matter what color you wish to paint it, two immoral choices will never make a moral one.

When life begins has now been well established to be at the moment of conception yet those who would disagree will argue that it is irrelevant for they claim that it is not when life begins that is of any importance but rather when a life becomes a person. The mental gymnastics used by some to define personhood are truly mind-boggling, abhorrent, decidedly immoral, and definitively intrinsically evil.

In one instance, two bioethicists, in a well-respected journal laid claim to this astounding bit of logical legerdemain: *"By showing that (1) both fetuses and newborns do not have the same moral status as actual persons, (2) the fact that both are potential persons is morally irrelevant, and (3) adoptions is not always in the best interest of actual people, the authors argue that what we call 'after-birth abortion' (killing a newborn) should be permissible in all cases where abortion is."*[10] The authors went further to define a newborn as any infant under the age of four!

My first reaction upon reading this piece of unctuous vomitus was to immediately and involuntarily disgorge the contents of my stomach. Inexplicably, far too many ascribe to this particularly grotesque point of view.

After a particularly difficult night I woke with a somewhat more pleasant thought, thinking of the experience shared by each of us yet

---

[10] A. Giubilini & F. Minerva, *"After-birth abortion: why should the baby live?"*, Journal of Medical Ethics, March 2012.

remembered by none, of that time when the entire universe which we know is confined to our mother's womb.

While what follows admittedly has no basis on personal memory or experience I cannot help but believe it is not particularly far from the truth, for though our mind and body may be incapable of cognitive thought or understanding in those earliest moments of our lives, the soul, created and installed by God at the moment of conception, comes into existence fully formed.

A long, long time ago,
much before I knew
of larger things,
I slept and
then I
dreamt.

I knew nothing beyond
the inviting womb
where I began
to grow and
grow and
grow.

When I heard soft murmurs
of sweet lullabies,
I felt somehow,
the music
was for
me.

*It was a pleasant time
floating without care
or worry there
not knowing;
growing
so.*

*What began so empty
over time grew small:
it left small space
to float or
even
move.*

*Yet I would often stretch
my limbs and against
the shrinking walls
would attempt
to make
room.*

*For the most part I slept
and dreamed pleasantly
it seemed to me
even though
nothing's
left.*

*A time came when I woke
with some urgency
knowing, sensing
something strange,
something
new.*

*My warm, inviting home
with waves of action
was suddenly
compelling
me to
leave.*

*Yet I did resist it,
what, I did not know,
yet I feared it,
for it was
squeezing
me.*

*It was so difficult
to resist the force
compelling me,
pushing me,
pulling
me.*

*I felt something touch me
and then suddenly
I was blinded
by a light
in my
eyes.*

The world that I had known
for so long was gone
there were no walls
I could move
freely
now.

And then I felt it, pain!
It hurt so I cried
the noise I heard
came from me,
from my
mouth.

So rudely awakened
from peaceful slumber
with sensations
new and so
I was
born.

And God Knows

Love never leaves

WHEN **GOD CALLS** someone we love into his loving arms, he leaves us with the memories of all which we have shared during our lives here on this earth. But above all else he leaves us all the love that was so much a part of our lives together. I am thoroughly convinced that this is so.

When I lost my parents unexpectedly in an automobile accident I experienced a wound so deep it took years to heal. It took even longer to fully understand that while I could no longer hold them, speak to them, or see them in any physical sense, I still heard and felt their love, now echoed through the love of those who knew them. I felt it through my siblings and their families, I felt it in the multitude of friends who recalled how much they loved them, but most of all I felt it within my mind and heart and soul. I knew I was loved and that in death their love had not died with them but continued to live on in countless ways.

When a dear friend's husband was tragically killed in an accident, I reached out to her in the only way I could at the time, by letting her know that while he might be out of sight their love would continue and endure.

> I was so deeply sorry to hear of your terrible loss. It seems like yesterday when I came face-to-face with the sudden deaths of my parents. Although it has been many years since their accident I still feel the pain of their loss and miss them terribly.
>
> I know so very well the pain and anguish you must be feeling right now and I only

wish I could provide a few words that could help you find some small measure of peace in his passing.

For me it was in knowing that mom and dad are kicking back and enjoying eternity with God. And I cannot help but believe that, while they were perfectly happy as things were, having the love of your life there with them to catch up on all the things that have been happening since their passing will undoubtedly bring them great joy.

*I cannot say I know how you must feel
for only God can see within your heart
… but God knows.*

*I cannot say your heart will ever mend
or regain some measure of your loss
… but God knows.*

*I know that God grants strength to each of us
in portions that He knows we each can bear
… yes God knows.*

*I know that true love does not leave
but lingers near and holds us close
… and God knows.*

*You know that love is never lost
but only waiting to be found again
… and God knows.*

Once Upon A Memory

Rich with love

MEMORIES are fickle notions, often so ephemeral they are lost before you have the opportunity to acknowledge their existence, while others endure for a lifetime, indelibly etched upon the pages of your mind. Then there are those memories which in truth are but chimeras, false memories conjured solely from your own imagination. And then there are real memories which over time have been embellished well beyond any possible actuality.

Standing at the foot of a tall mountain, the eye of a climber will focus completely on its peak without seeing or considering the broad vistas and the beauty that lay beyond. Standing upon the highest point, the climber cannot easily discern the starting point, now hidden below the clouds, and the eyes no longer view the world from such a narrow lens; rather, the view has become panoramic, overwhelming the senses with the majesty of it all. As the climber ascends the mountain, what is seen will differ depending on the climber's point of view, whether looking up at the peak or down toward the valley far below.

Life and our memories of it are much the same. The young see nothing but today, for tomorrow is beyond their knowing and the past beyond undoing. The old greet today in gratitude for the gift of waking to another day and the past holds rich memories to occupy the present.

When does the climber realize the mountain top is nearer than its base? When does the eye shift its focus from the goal to the vistaed beauty that surrounds? Seldom will the climber find a sign post which informs how far the climb or how much further to the top.

The same is true in life for there never comes a moment when we encounter a sign that announces the approach or crossing of that great divide which marks the passage from young to old.

We are older now than just before and younger than a moment more; the difference is in where we are on our journey from its beginning to eternity.

Seldom will admission come from either young or old of what virtues may be obtained from reaching out to one another. This is truly sad, for in listening to the old the young who lack experience could readily acquire the wisdom of those who have a lifetime of experience. And the old could rediscover a sense of purpose and a renewed interest in living outside their memories.

*Life that once sprang from a womb
so like a bloom in early spring
to face the sun and breathe the air,
an innocent so fragile born
will all too soon fly from the nest
when summer smiles and warms the heart
and life itself is rich with love.*

*Age that once was yet to come
unimagined for one so young
no doubt the sun would always shine
and Camelot was not a dream.
Sudden now have the years ahead
brushed the past with indifference
like leaves that bend to autumn's wind.*

*Hands that once wore soft and smooth
now share the scars of labors past
from holding tight to daring dreams
which in their youth did dare to dream
all was possible, great and small,
now so gently hold tiny hands
yet unblemished by passing years.*

Feet that once paved untried paths
with sure and steady confidence
striding forth with merciless pace
to reach far beyond heaven's gate
for the prize so earnestly sought
now do step with uncertain gait
to walk across the smallest space.

Eyes that once did love invite
and sparkled with smiling laughter
yet undimmed by grief and sorrow
or clouded by unbidden pain
from wounds inflicted, scars so deep
no soothing aloe will erase
such evidence of aching loss.

Ears that once knew sweet music
that did arrive from virgin lips
with unrequited melody
upon the yet unbroken heart
which had not yet felt passion's loss
or felt the emptiness that fills
the soul when love forever dies.

Lips that once touched tender lips
and tasted love's sweet devotion
for the breathless flight of passion
which gave flame to emotion's fire
burning all thought and care away
desiring nothing but release
from such relentless agony.

Love that once waxed poetic
with pubescent understanding
driven by raw youthful passion
seeking, searching, wanting, needing
that which was desired but knew not
of that which was so greatly sought
knowing it was not love at all.

Memories that once were dreams
and destinations yet arrived
now fill the soul with distant tunes
and all the countless reveries
which made the journey so complete.
An autumn chill is in the air
winter's frost is fast approaching.

Echoes of Love

How will I know?

IN the 1965 movie Shenandoah there is a scene which resonated with me then and has remained with me these many years. Set during the American Civil War, a widower with six sons and one daughter, Charlie Anderson (Jimmy Stewart) is sitting on his front porch preparing to smoke a cigar when his daughter's suitor, Lieutenant Sam (Doug McClure) approaches and asks for his daughter's hand in marriage. Charlie responds by asking *"Why? Why do you want to marry her?"* When Sam responds *"Well, I love her"* Charlie tells him *"That's not good enough. Do you like her?"* to which Sam starts to say *"I just said I..."*

only to be interrupted by Charlie who tells him *"No, no. You just said you loved her. There's some difference between lovin' and likin'. When I married Jennie's mother, I-I didn't love her - I liked her... I liked her a lot. I liked Martha for at least three years after we were married and then one day it just dawned on me I loved her. I still do... still do. You see, Sam, when you love a woman without likin' her, the night can be long and cold, and contempt comes up with the sun."*

There is indeed *"some difference between lovin' and likin'"* as Charlie Anderson says, although far too many fail to see it or purposely avoid acknowledging the difference when they enter into a relationship, especially a life-long, forever relationship such as marriage. Furthermore, they seldom see the absolute necessity for both loving someone and liking them as well.

It is our egoism that gets in the way, our selfish desires, our overpowering conceit, and our self-interest that keeps us focused inwardly on ourselves rather than outwardly on any other. In our myopic self-centric universe, where everything revolves around the core being of self, nothing, even God—who is seldom given any thought or consideration at all—stands in subservience to one's own godhood. Life, other than our own, is of value only as long as it serves our needs, our wants, and our desires. When it no longer satisfies it is casually dismissed, cast off as so much useless detritus, without a single moment's thought.

The reason we don't know the difference between *lovin'* and *likin'* is because we have no true understanding of what either truly means. We are quite comfortable in our self-proclaimed godhood and have no desire to expose the fact that the *"emperor has no clothes."*

Simply put, we enjoy the self-imposed fog which hides any semblance of truth from our vanity and our conceit. As long as we are happy little else matters. We studiously avoid engaging in open-minded intellectual pursuits, such as studying serious works of philosophy, ethics, morality, faith, or God. Instead we actively pursue only that which can provide instant pleasure and thus we avoid any unwanted and unnecessary confrontation with the realities of life.

It is only when we let go of our egoistic concerns and begin to love others as God loves (*agape*), with an unconditional love that we can truly know what it is to love. But in order to truly love someone for a life-time, you must first like (*philia*) them and you must be willing to share your entire self with them. And yes, it does make a difference.

*Give me but a moment dear
and let me catch a thought or two,
so I may answer truthfully
to what you have inquired of me.*

*What you ask is difficult
because it means so many things
but I will try my very best
to set your heart and mind to rest.*

*You asked me how you would know
when cupid's arrow pierced your heart
and whether what you felt was true
or simply passion passing through.*

*Let me respond in this way:
true love is rarely found today
for love is seldom understood
to be the kind of love it should.*

*Forever love does warm the heart
but it is never what you feel
or how you suddenly cannot
utter a single cogent thought.*

*What so many think as love
is really something else, you see,
for passion plays a selfish song
which seldom lasts for very long.*

*Love appears reluctantly
it dares not trample virgin soil
for love must bloom in air and light
from friendship grown love takes flight.*

*A love that lasts forever more
thru all that life will throw your way
must be a love you give away,
yes, all of it, every day.*

*When you love another more
than even your own life you see
you will forfeit every part:
your soul, your spirit and your heart.*

*When you love someone enough
to lose yourself in the other,
you will want to be together,
united now and forever.*

*To truly love another
demands the utmost devotion
to the other, without measure
for the other is your treasure.*

*Remember love will prevail
thru all that life will throw at you
as long as you consider love
a gift from God sent from above.*

*Love is like a winding path
which hides itself beneath the leaves
curving aimlessly, to and fro
what lies ahead we cannot know.*

*Love can weather any storm
overcome any obstacle
for whatever life throws at you
love will prevail if it is true.*

*Standing on a mountain top
gazing long upon such beauty
wondering why, God only knows
yet love returns to us in echoes.*

*Echoes of love, you will hear
when all your love you give away
yet know that if your love is true
much more will be returned to you.*

From A Distance

Forever side by side

FOREVER love lasts forever, far beyond the distance vowed by *"until death do us part"* for love resides in the soul which we know will continue long after our mortal bodies have returned to dust.

There is an emptiness that invades the heart upon the passing of one's beloved. The pain of loss is all too real and the loneliness is often more than the heart can bear. But the worst is the silence where once there was laughter; it breaks the spirit, releasing all the grief and sorrow in agonizing waves.

Simple things, so familiar, even habitual, suddenly become difficult or impossible to acknowledge or accept. Simple things, performed over a lifetime, like walking through the door at the end of the day or listening to the breathing of that special someone sleeping beside you every night.

Yet the absence doesn't mean you are alone. Forever love never ends; it ascends, becoming something more, far beyond what we mortals can conceive or comprehend.

Those who believe in an invisible, unknowable, all-loving God should understand that death is not the end but the beginning of eternal life. In truth, life as we experience it, can be viewed as a brief gestation period, a time of development and growth, and like the caterpillar in its cocoon, we will be transformed from what we now are in this life into something far more beautiful which will live forever. Each of us is created with a body and a soul and while the body may no longer live, the soul, our spirit will live on for all eternity.

Although now unencumbered by earthly restraint, the spirit will remain united with your soul and will always know what is in your heart and the love that lives within your soul. You cannot hide from your beloved any more than you can hide from God.

If you can believe that this is so, then take the time to listen as if your beloved were by your side. Smile and enjoy the moment as if your love were with you now. For you are the one so truly blessed knowing that the one you love and the one who has loved you for so long will never leave you.

Embrace each moment until you meet again in the spirit. Speak of familiar things with love and love will always respond with more love.

*The silence of your laughter
echoes softly thru the air
stirring quiet memories
of your smile and gentle kiss,
of sunshine that would follow
when you walked into the room
to whisper soft "I love you"
for no reason, just because.*

*Oh sweet love I will remain
ever near your loving heart
closer than I've ever been
for my spirit loves you still
and I will forever be
here beside you, ever near
whispering soft "I love you"
forever love, just for you.*

*What sweet longing does instruct
my heart to take great comfort
in knowing you are keeping
watch with such strict vigilance
and unceasing devotion,
yet I cannot dare admit
what desire I would request
would you again be near me.*

*I know my love, yes I know
what emptiness now resides
within your heart still beating
with a passion yet undimmed
and a love forever vowed
on an oath never broken,
what God, by his grace, did bless
even death can't separate.*

Sitting here before the fire
reminiscing of the times
we watched the dancing firelight
glimmer in the other's eyes
telling tales of love profound
where words lay on silent lips,
unspoken thoughts understood
with but a glance between us.

Sit before the fire awhile
while I whisper to your heart:
there will be more tomorrows
you will never be alone
for I am with you always
as I promised I would be
when first I knew I loved you
long before eternity.

What memories do invade
these fortress walls where I hide
all the sorrow and the pain
buried deep 'neath weighty stone
for I cannot bear the thought
of one more day sitting here
staring at these silent walls
wishing you were by my side.

Let your sorrow rest with me
for my spirit knows not pain,
no hunger, fear, or regrets
beyond this brief interlude
where what is and what shall be
by mortal eyes must remain
hidden by the veil of time
yet my spirit does remain.

*The silence that now pervades
what once was filled with laughter
serves to amplify the sound
of time in somber beating
to the tempo of a dirge;
a slow mournful elegy
echoing down empty halls
in endless repetition.*

*Close your eyes and remember
all the times we were apart
yet our love and happiness
proved the power of the heart
to dismiss the chasmed miles
as if we sat side by side
holding hands with tenderness
rather than so far away.*

Memories I must confess
make me smile and laugh a bit
at the whole we made of it
the better one out of two
the sum of us greater than
what one and one could attain
for God filled our souls with love
and kept us safe in his arms.

Oh my love you understand
what death but a brief remove,
for death will greet one and all
from such chill grasp no reprieve
yet there is beyond the grave
so much more the soul to find
than our mortal eyes can see
and love, my love, never ends.

*Yes, my love, I know it's true
though chasmed depths now divide
when once we were together;
should I need now tarry here
for a while or longer still
my heart will ache all the more
but my soul will feel your breath
whisper soft beside me still.*

*In the silence that pervades,
let your soul in solitude
find comfort in the stillness;
let you spirit find that place
where we can be together,
for I am always with you
no matter what time or place
even when you feel alone.*

Of Love

What beauty do truths betray

WHAT LOVE is has confounded we mortal beings from the very beginning. Far too many of us have convinced ourselves that we know what love is, while in truth, only God knows and while he has given us the gift and the grace to know love, he has never stopped us from making a total mess of it.

There are many who if given a verbal Rohrschach test to say the first word that comes to mind when they hear the word "love" would undoubtedly respond with "sex". From a cultural perspective that appears to be the preponderant view these days. It is indeed profoundly sad to think that so many conflate mindless animal rutting with a gift uniquely given to us by God.

All living things procreate in some form or fashion but only humanity has been gifted with the capacity to love one another so intimately. To conflate love and sex is not only wrong but morally bankrupt.

Love, and here we a speaking of self-sacrificing, selfless, self-giving love, is not easy to find or hold on to and perhaps that is what drives so many to accept such a poor substitute as momentary pleasure. Those who lack the will to diligently search for someone to whom they honestly desire to love above all else, more even than themselves, too often choose sex as a poor substitute for love.

God gave us love and showed us what it means to love another by sending his only son to live among us and to suffer and die, to give his life out of love for us. That is agape, that is love without measure, that is the love we are meant to emulate and to share with another.

Only when we love enough to give all that we have for the benefit of another without expecting or desiring anything in return will we truly know love. Only when we love so much that our heart aches at the very thought of our beloved will we know what truths reside in our love.

When we feel loved, that feeling comes from the one who loves us in return, not because we want it, desire it or have asked for it, but because the one you love loves you in the same way.

Three loves become one love, for never forget that God is love and always, always is a co-equal partner in our love.

Of love, what beauty do truths betray
when kindred spirits stay temptation,
forsaking momentary pleasure
to obtain what may ne'er be stolen
but must be given without purchase
for what must be bought is never love,
a brief delusion and nothing more.

On love, from what river does it flow
with such abandon no pow'r may tame;
what trickling wellspring is the handmaid,
a womb unblemished, a soul unstained;
ever does a single raindrop fall
with such purpose, divinely given,
what purpose ours but to love our God.

For love, what prayer on bended knee
in ardent hope would supplicate,
so to suborn what tender mercies
have yet to offer with devotion
forever love without condition;
a captive bird will sing in silence
and love so contrived will never be.

*In love, with what passion love enjoins
the serenade written on the heart
to be, with true faith and devotion,
performed with perfect admiration;
for such attention to the music,
when so sweetly played, lifts the spirit
of the soul above the clouds to soar.*

*With love, no greater want should attend
than the measure of what is given
without remark or contemplation
but for the welfare of the other;
strange the notion, giving gifts away,
with no advantage or merit gained,
but the knowing of it is enough.*

*Why love, what soul dares to open wide
the heart to chance it may be broken,
shattered and abandoned, lost, alone?
Yet the soul dares love beyond the self
for the soul is incomplete alone,
it must be richly fed, filled with love,
a gift of self, selflessly given.*

*When love, on a fresh breeze surprises
with sweet scents to tickle the senses
and nightingales serenade so soft,
when in the moment least expected
comes a vision of beauty perfect,
to light by flickering candlelight
a fire within the heart, embrace it.*

*Where love, from what treasury obtained
this jewel so great, so undeserved,
a gift bestowed without condition
by a love so divine, out of love
for creatures mirrored, all reflections
of love unbounded with free accord,
to love their God and one another.*

*Come love, what duty is demanded,
what great consequence does love provoke,
what is required for love requited?
To be loved, give love, for what is love
but a gift of grace from Love Divine,
never may the heart e'er long possess,
for love's a gift that must be given.*

I Believe

In the One I love

NO LOVE is greater than the love of God. Out of his boundless, infinite love God created everything and gifted it to those created in his own image and likeness. He asked for nothing in return, yet we owe God a debt we can never hope to repay for he gave us everything.

I frequently remind my religious education students that God loves us, no matter what happens in our lives. It makes no difference whether we want it, whether we ask for it, or whether we believe that we deserve it, He still loves us. We are His children; He created us in his image. Henri Nouwen once said that *"we are not loved by God because we are precious, but we are precious because we are loved by God."*

True love does not come from within us; it comes from God. You cannot know love through the external; it cannot be found in a book or a lecture; it must be experienced by living and loving God. We live in a world that has little time for God, little time for love; it is because we know so little of God that we fail to find true love.

I further remind my students that we owe God our love in return. He created us out of love and you have to love Him for our creation. Up to this point all heads are usually nodding in agreement. But then comes the kicker. Since God created us out of love and we must love Him, we must also love God's creation, all of it, most importantly, every person created by God. If you don't love others then how can you truly love God?

Loving others is seldom easy and it often comes with a heavy price. Certainly God paid dearly with the death of His only Son on the cross, so we must expect to pay the price if we love God and love others. We may face rejection and abuse, perhaps even suffering or death, but if you love God you have no choice but to love your neighbor as yourself. Dr. Michael Duduit, Executive Editor of **Preaching** magazine writes that *"The life of love is not an easy or a common one, but it is the road that leads to Christ."*

God's love for us is manifested through Jesus who died so that we could know God's love. God so loved the world that he sent His only son, Jesus Christ, who became man, suffered, died, and rose for the forgiveness of sin and the salvation of the whole world. Everyone is included, no exceptions. God loves us all, even those who might not believe in Him. Jesus said, *"I have other sheep that do not belong to this fold. These also I must lead, and they will hear my voice, and there will be one flock, one shepherd."*[11] God runs an "all inclusive" club; everyone is invited and welcome to join.

---

[11] Jn 10:16.

Jesus has told us *"I am the good shepherd."*[12] References to shepherds can be found throughout the bible. Kings, and those in leadership positions, both political and religious, are often metaphorically spoken of as shepherds of their people. It is a reference that is generally understood and accepted.

However, especially today, most of us respond negatively if we are called sheep. We think of sheep as timid creatures, not very bright, easily fooled by wolves in sheep's clothing, led like lambs to the slaughter. The imagery is just not very appealing, to say the least.

But, in the English language, sheep have a rather singular distinction, because the word has no singular, only the plural. Sheep belong to a flock, following a shepherd who they trust to keep them safe. The shepherd knows his flock and as Jesus tells us *"I am the good shepherd, and I know mine and mine know me, just*

---

[12] Jn 10:11.

as the Father knows me and I know the Father; and I will lay down my life for the sheep."[13]

To be a Christian means we belong to Christ, the good shepherd, and it means we belong together, not as individuals, but as a community of believers who share in the body of Christ and our love for one another.

But…does that have to include everyone, even those who aren't, you know, like us? After all, if they aren't with us they must be against us, right? How can they be included when they don't believe everything that we believe? If they aren't part of our community of believers then they can't be loved by God quite as much as we are.

But the truth is that it is not up to us to decide who is in or who is out. Jesus tells us that *"I have other sheep that do not belong to this fold. These also I must lead, and they will hear my voice, and there will be one flock, one shepherd."*[14] The

---

[13] Jn 10:14-15.
[14] Jn 10:16.

Good Shepherd loves all, leads all, not just our flock.

But if everyone is invited, who will be included? Jesus tells us *"For I was hungry and you gave me food, I was thirsty and you gave me drink, a stranger and you welcomed me, naked and you clothed me, ill and you cared for me, in prison and you visited me."*[15]

So, what are we to do? For starters, like Jesus, we must open our hearts and arms to everyone; we must love our neighbor as our self; we must love everyone as our Heavenly Father loves each of us; for, if we love the stranger, we will soon discover that the stranger is no longer strange, but our brother or sister.

When we look at others through the eyes of Christ we will see, as in a mirror, a reflection of our self—the image and likeness of God.

---

[15] Mt 25:35-36.

*I believe
that God is there and here and everywhere,
that God is then and now and forever.*

*That we,
despite our faults and failures,
despite our arrogance and pride,
despite our anger and our hate
are loved by our Creator God
because we are his creation,
because we are his children,
because we are his and his alone.*

*Therefore I will sing praises
to the One who created me,
to the One who gives me life,
to the One who is my Father,
to the One who loves me,
to the One I love.*

The Bonds Of Love
Keep silent watch

THERE is often a mist of poetry to be found within common prose, a phrase that sings a melody, a line that beats with the rhythm of a metered verse, or a passage that somehow transcends its purpose and breaks the bonds of ordinary composition. Unintended though it may have been, somehow thoughts that lie within the heart and soul burst forth with such beauty that it takes your breath away.

Early in the year 1985 I found myself reading miscellaneous notes written by my mother. They were mostly thoughts and ideas that she had saved for a purpose yet to be determined and that now would never find the light of day for we had lost our parents on January 16th, 1985 in a terrible accident. As I perused the scraps of paper lying on her desk I came upon one sheet that appeared to be more than a momentary thought, more complete than most of the notes that I had found and it spoke to me of a love that cannot be measured and of a love that has become far too rare these days.

What she wrote was of two trees which stood in front of their home, an autumn day, the color of the leaves and, in a subtle way, the cycle of life. Yet those of us who knew her most intimately, her children, read in her words, prose that waxed poetic, verse which revealed bonds of love so strong and yet so gentle, a union that had survived war, depression, and difficulties few today could ever know or understand. It spoke of the silent watch my parents so lovingly kept over each other all the many years they were together. Though they were different in many ways, they were truly kindred souls whose love transcended the ordinary to become a love so extraordinary.

The hickory and the cedar still stand tall outside the windows of our parent's country home. They keep silent watch over those who come to visit and remember. Three generations still come to stand silently and hear their voices whisper "I love you" as they have always done. They are bound together, supporting each other, loving each other for now and forever.

I have taken the liberty; perhaps a bit presumptuous on my part I must admit, but certainly with the greatest love and admiration, to include my mother's thoughts as the final poem in this work. Had it been my dad doing this, I can hear with perfect clarity my mother's response, knowing so well her gentle, unassuming and humble manner. She would, with a gentle smile upon her face and a twinkle in her eye, simply say, "*Oh, Bob!*"

I love and miss you both.

The hills and trees were fantastic.
Everyone seemed to agree
it was one of the most
beautiful autumns ever.

I wish I could put the color
of the trees to paper.
In that respect, the painter
has an advantage over the writer.

Still, I doubt if any painter
ever put such color to canvas
as the woods
have displayed this year.

But even as the colors have faded,
day by day,
Nature's other beauties take over.

Most of the brilliant leaves are gone.
The oak's brown hangs on,
like an old bag lady
of the forest's streets.

*The goldenrod has turned
a fragile gray,
each delicate clump hanging
on a leafless stem.*

*It snowed last Sunday,
and every weed became a jewel,
every tree a miracle.*

*The cedar below the yard
was capped with snow,
and its companion, a hickory,
thrust its snow-tipped naked branches
into a wintry sky.*

*Someone suggested
we should cut the cedar.*

Oh, no!

*The two of them
seem bound together,
supporting each other.*

*During the summer and fall,
the hickory stands out,
first green with youth
and then golden
as the year ages,
but in winter,
the cedar,
which has seemed
unimportant all year,
comes into its own.*

*It gives us the green
of hope all year.*

*It promises that,
come spring,
those bare lined trees
now unable
to hide their nakedness,
will again
be clothed
in splendor.*

*I keep harkening back
to the beauty of the leaves
this fall.*

*Walking down the road,
I felt like
I was in a child's paint box,
with the colors splashing
all around me.*

*Even the oaks,
which usually turn
a deadly dull brown,
this year,
were a velvet burgundy,
and every hill
was aflame
with red and gold.*

Life is so peaceful here.

About the Author

Charles (Chuck) R. Lanham was ordained into the Permanent Diaconate September 17, 2011. It has been a long and often tortuous road.

Deacon Chuck continues to serve the parish of Saint Albert the Great Catholic Community of the Diocese of Reno, Nevada. He is the Director of Adult Faith Formation and Homebound Ministries for the parish, conducts frequent adult faith formation workshops, and is a regular homilist. He currently serves as the bulletin editor for the parish bulletin.

He continues writing a weekly column intended to encompass a broad landscape of thoughts and ideas on matters of theology, faith, morals, teachings of the magisterium and the Catholic Church; they are meant to illuminate, illustrate, and catechize the readers and now number more than 200 articles. All his reflections, homilies, and commentaries are posted and can be found on his website: http://deaconscorner.org. Comments are always welcome and appreciated.

Deacon Chuck is the author of **The Voices of God: hearing God in the silence** which offers the reader insights into how to hear God's voice through all of the noise that surrounds us.

Happily married to Janet for over forty-seven years, they have two daughters and five grandchildren.

He holds undergraduate degrees in History & Political Science, and Business Administration, and a graduate degree in Computer Science. He is a Vietnam Veteran, serving in the U.S. Army for nine years. He has worked at several large computer and software companies, and as an entrepreneur founded three startup companies.

He is the author of numerous technical papers and books and shares a patent for a remote monitoring device.

He lives in Reno, Nevada, just minutes away from the shores of Lake Tahoe, where he is convinced that you cannot get much closer to heaven than there.

He regularly speaks to groups of all ages and sizes and would welcome the opportunity to speak to your group.

If you would like to be placed on a mailing list for future books or would like to have him speak to your group, email:

Deacon.Chuck@deaconscorner.org.

Bibliography

Unlike my previous book, **The Voices of God**, this book is essentially my own, largely devoid of referenced works by other authors and sources.

While I am a Christian of the Roman Catholic tradition and this work acknowledges and professes my firm faith in God the Father, Son and Holy Spirit, it is my hope that those of other faiths and beliefs will still find favor in its reading.

What follows is a brief list of referenced works which I hope you will enjoy as much as I have enjoyed reading them.

A Morally Complex World:
Engaging Contemporary Moral Theology,
James T. Bretzke, S.J., Liturgical Press, 2004.

Casti Connubii, Encyclical Letter,
Pope Pius XI, December 31, 1930.

Catechism of the Catholic Church Second Edition,
Libreria Editrice Vaticana. 1994.

Discernment:
Reading the signs of daily life,
Henri J. M. Nouwen. HarperCollins Publishers. 2013.

Fundamentals of the Faith:
Essays in Christian Apologetics,
Peter Kreeft. Ignatius Press. 1988.

Humanae Vitae, Encyclical Letter,
Pope Paul VI, July 25, 1968.

Intimacy,
Henri J. M. Nouwen. HarperCollins Publishers. 1969.

Making Choices:
Practical wisdom for everyday moral decisions,
Peter Kreeft. Servant Books. 1990.

The New American Bible: Saint Joseph Edition,
Catholic Book Publishing Corp., New York, 1992.

The Inner Voice of Love:
A journey through anguish to freedom,
Henri J. M. Nouwen. Doubleday, 1998.

The Return of the Prodigal Son:
A story of homecoming,
Henri J. M. Nouwen, Doubleday, Aug. 6, 1994.

To Live is to Love:
Meditations on love and Spirituality,
Ernesto Cardenal, Herder and Herder, 1972.

Veritas Splendor, Encyclical Letter,
Pope Saint John Paul II, August 6, 1993

www.ingramcontent.com/pod-product-compliance
Lightning Source LLC
Chambersburg PA
CBHW070550050426
42450CB00011B/2798